IGNORE THE "NO!"

IGNORE THE "NO!"

Empower Yourself to Do the Impossible!

REV. DR. STEPHEN ALBERT

Waterside Productions

Copyright © 2023 by Rev. Dr. Stephen Albert

All rights reserved. This book or any portion thereof may not be reproduced or used in any manner whatsoever without the express written permission of the publisher except for the use of brief quotations in articles and book reviews.

ISBN-13: 978-1-958848-76-0 print edition
ISBN-13: 978-1-958848-77-7 e-book edition

Waterside Productions

2055 Oxford Ave
Cardiff, CA 92007
www.waterside.com

Dedication

This book is dedicated to everyone
who was once told "NO!"
and believed it.
I'm sorry it happened to you;
Now Let's HEAL!

To my Love, Abigail,
who helped me through
all my many "NO!s"

Thank You God.

TABLE OF CONTENTS

Preface ·· 1

Impossible? ··· 5
My First "NO!" ····································· 6
I Wish I Had! ······································ 12
"Chutzpah" ·· 14
"Why Me Lord?" ·································· 17
Attitude ·· 19
Rebooting To "Yes!" ······························ 21
Your Future ······································· 24
An Unexpected "NO!" ···························· 30
Let's Be Honest ··································· 33
Speaking About Miracles ························ 37
The Use of Previous Thought ··················· 40
Meditation ··· 43
When "NO!" is the Answer! ····················· 50

About the Author ································· 57
Endorsers Who Ignored The "NO!" ············ 61

Preface

Since the time we first began to crawl, someone was there to tell us "NO!"

The first "NO!" we ever heard was probably said in a very loving/protective way to make sure we didn't get hurt; but the effect on our brain was the same as telling us not to try for something we wanted. STOP! DON'T GO NEAR THAT! BE CAREFUL! NOOOOO! UH-UH! THAT'S HOT! DON'T RUN IN THE HOUSE! THAT'S SHARP! YOU'LL GET HURT!!!

A child's curiosity is normal and expected. It is part of the learning process. As long as it is done safely, a child expanding his or her barriers should be celebrated. Over the early years of childhood, we learned that certain actions on our part could result in our possibly falling or getting hurt by touching a sharp object or a hot utensil or anything else which would make us cry or call out for an adult to come rescue us.

"NO!" is an easy word to say and most children hear it so much, they pick up that word when they begin to talk. "Do you want a cookie? the parent asks. "NO!" the child says as he or she reaches for the cookie. "Do you want to wear the blue shirt? "NO!" the child says as he or she points to the blue shirt.

The word "NO!" somehow offers us a perceived degree of power and puts us in charge of the situation for that moment.

Throughout our childhood, the word "NO!" was used over and over and over again to shield us and to reduce the chance of our feeling we failed when trying something new. Depending on the authoritative figures in our life, our actions and thinking were directed by sometimes over-protective people. Proper parenting includes allowing the child to make a mistake, to fall down every now and then. This is how we learn to get through life's more difficult moments. However, sometimes we hold on to the "NOs!" and they limit our trying anything for fear that we might fail or do it incorrectly.

This book is about how we can go beyond all the "NOs" we received early in life and eliminate any barriers which we may have created in our mind when we want to try something new.

"It's Kind Of Fun To Do The Impossible"
Walt Disney

Stephen King's first writing "Carrie" received 30 "Nos" before it was published. Dr. Seuss' book "Horton Hears A Who!" was published after 27 "NOs". J.K. Rowling received 12 "Nos" for her first book "Harry Potter and the Philosopher's Stone."

IGNORE THE "NO!"

***If the Impossible is Possible
<u>in Our Mind</u>,
then We Can Expect Miracles
to Develop
After Each Impossibility
Is Conquered.***

Rev. Dr. Stephen Albert

Impossible?

It doesn't take a genius to realize that most of the inventions and luxuries which we enjoy today, began in the mind of people who were told, "WHAT ARE YOU CRAZY? IT'LL <u>NEVER</u> Work!" In Jeane Manning's book, "Top 10 Impossible Inventions that Work" Manning identifies that:

- The English Academy of Science laughed at Benjamin Franklin when he re-ported his discovery of the lightning rod, and the Academy refused to publish his report.
- A gathering of German engineers in 1902 ridiculed Count Ferdinand Von Zeppelin for claiming to invent a steerable balloon. (Later, Zeppelin airships flew commercially across the Atlantic.)
- Major newspapers ignored the historic 1903 flight of the Wright brother's airplane because Scientific American suggested the flight was a hoax, and for five years officials in Washington, D.C. did not believe that the heavier-than-air machine had flown.

Thomas Edison and the Light Bulb, Horace Rackham and the "Horseless Carriage," John Logie Baird and the Television, Charles Babbage and the Computer, J.C.R. Licklider and the Internet, and on and on, all heard the word "NO!" said to them over and over and over again.

My First "NO!"

I was a very lucky kid. I was born in 1947 into a family which allowed for mistakes. Our small one-way street of rowhouses in West Philadelphia had very few obstacles and I was allowed to explore the many options open to me often unaware that my mother was probably watching from a nearby obscure location. On my own at 4, I fell on my knee while running in an alley and it required 2 stitches at the doctor's office. I do not remember anyone telling me to never run again. The message was, "Be Careful" but there were few "Nos!"

I grew up during a time when kids jumped on their bikes after breakfast on a Saturday and were expected home before it got dark. One day we experimented with potentially dangerous science kits in a kid's basement; we created forts in nearby forest areas, we built a miniature golf course on a vacant lot; and without fear, we walked to the movie house 6 blocks away on Saturday to see the cartoons and feature film. As we got a little older, we took local busses and subways by ourselves to downtown Philadelphia stores and museums, and we explored many places in which we heard nearby adult's shout, "You kids get out of here!" But there were few "Nos!"

Then in 1964 I experienced my first big "NO." It was delivered to me by my high school college counselor at the end of my junior year. Mrs. Reyburne interviewed each student, one at a time, and questioned them as to their plans after high school. This was a no-brainer discussion for me because of my great desire to be an architect. In the drafting class I was taking at the time, while the other kids were drawing front and side views of some object, I was designing, drawing and submitting floor plans for homes.

When Mrs. Reyburne asked me, "So what do you want to do after high school?" I quickly answered, "I want to be an architect!" Her response was, **"NO,"** you cannot be an architect; like becoming a doctor, it is a very difficult field to get into and your grades are not high enough." "Stephen," she said, "you are not college material. Perhaps you should think about a drafting program at a technical school." I looked at her and in no uncertain terms I said forcefully, "I Want To Be An Architect!" She repeated, "Stephen, you are not college material."

Looking back now I don't know if I fulfilled my dreams of becoming an architect BECAUSE I was told "NO!" or if my strong desire and my abilities meshed in some predetermined way orchestrated by God. (I choose to believe the latter.) I earned 3 college degrees and I TAUGHT college for 44 years. I was an Architect for 25 years and I designed over 450 retail stores throughout the world.

Mrs. Reyburne was wrong; and I have always wondered how many other kids who had a dream for their life, left those dreams on her office floor after hearing her say the word "NO!"

If You Can Overcome "NO!" Once…

After completing my Associates Degree in Engineering at Penn State, while working for architectural offices part time, I entered Drexel University's Bachelor's program in Architecture. When I was ready to go into my final year of study, I attended a Futures conference in Washington D.C. Barbara Marx Hubbard was one of the keynote speakers and I will never forget her words:

"If you have a dream that brings you JOY, and if you do the work, the infinite can manifest."

Those words led me to create in my mind a national Futures conference in Philadelphia called '2020 Visions of the Community'. I was the President of the Drexel Architectural student body, and I led the many student groups in the various architectural and art schools in Philadelphia. When I presented my potential conference at a student meeting, the feedback was less than warm. "We've never done anything that big before!" "We've just put on small local conferences every now and then, not something national!" The response by almost all the other students was **"NO!"**

I believed that what I was proposing was for the benefit of all. And I also realized that I could not do this alone. So, I developed a way to gather students from more than just the architectural and arts schools. I created a 3-semester INTERDISCINPLINARY college course which would blend students from other fields of study with architectural students. The course was called "The New City" and it would bring students together to plan cities of the Future. I surprised myself by getting some early student backing from various fields of study. Now all I had to do was convince Drexel University to run the program.

One evening I went to the Dean of Architecture and told him of my plans. I showed him the 3-semester interdisciplinary curriculum I had developed and asked him if we could offer it through the Architectural Department. He was Impressed ... and **he said "NO!"** He told me that he did not have the authority to develop a new program of this magnitude and that I should present this to the Dean of Drexel's Evening School.

So, I went to the Dean of the Evening School and told him of my plans. He was impressed ... and **he said "NO!"** He told me that creating an interdisciplinary program like this was way over his head. He did not have the authority to do it. He did however have an important suggestion. He told me to first get a tenured faculty member to co-teach it with me. Then there would be a better chance of it being accepted by the "higher ups."

I believe that if you want to do something good and you can persevere after hearing the word "NO!" said enough times, the universe will open doors that otherwise would remain closed. It just so happened that Dr. Arthur Shostak was a tenured professor in Drexel's Sociology Department and was also a Futurist. Unknown to me, he had spoken at the same conference in Washington D.C. which I had attended a few weeks before. So, I called him, and he agreed to meet with me for a cup of coffee.

Dr. Shostak earned his PhD at Princeton University and had taught at Drexel for nine years. He had authored more than 200 articles and authored or co-authored thirty-four books. He was a "higher up!" I showed him the 3-semester interdisciplinary curriculum I had developed and asked him if we could offer it through the Sociology Department. He was impressed... and **he said "NO!"** As tenured as he was, he did not have the authority to create a new course, let alone an interdisciplinary one. "But" however he said, "I would like to show this to the Dean of Sociology."

Dr. Shostak set up the meeting with his Dean two days later in the late morning. He told the Dean that he would be happy to teach the course and he wanted me to co-teach it. [Remember, I did not even have my bachelor's degree yet!] The Dean of Sociology looked over the curriculum and he was impressed. And **he said "NO!"** He told us that creating an interdisciplinary program like this was way over his head. He did not have the authority to do so.

So, with my head down in frustration, I asked him, "WHO DOES?"

He said, "The Dean of Curriculums is the only person who can authorize a course like this." So, I asked him, "What is the Dean's name and where can I find him?" The Dean said, "Oh, his office is on the second floor of the administration building across the street; but it may take you a few weeks to get an appointment with him." I looked at the Dean and Dr. Shostak and said, "Wait here; I will be right back."

I ran across the street, into the administration building and up the grand staircase to the second floor. The Dean's office was directly in front of me, and I walked in. Just as the secretary began to ask, "Can I help you?" the dean came out of his office directly behind her desk ready to go to lunch. We looked at each other; I ignored the secretary and with a surprised look on the Dean's face I said to him, "Sir, may I have 5 minutes of your time?" He said, "SURE!" He escorted me into his office, I presented the program including the many relevant "Yes Buts" I had received, and he looked at the material. Within five minutes the Dean approved the class!

I thanked him and ran back across the street to the Dean of Sociology and Dr. Shostak still sitting together in the Dean's office. Seeing the look of astonishment on their faces when I told them to call the Dean and he would give them a course number, was worth all the "NOs" I had received.

Dr. Shostak and I taught "The New City" for 3 semesters beginning in the Fall of 1975. Our roster of over 30 students included those from Science, Engineering, Architecture, Food Service, English, Nursing, Math, Fashion Design and a few other departments. In interdisciplinary teams, the students had fun developing cities of the future with no limits. The caveat was, if you designed a city with no jails, what would you do with people who commit crimes? If you wanted a city with flying cars, how would you handle traffic flow? Every decision had to be considered and judged for possible consequences. The classes were fun, imaginative and very challenging.

The 2020 Visions of the Community 3-day national conference that followed was a success. 500 people attended. Not knowing what I was doing, I asked everyone I knew to chip in. EVERYONE SAID, "YES!" Invitations to the event were mailed out free by local companies. A free, two-page spread of the events filled a local newspaper. Architectural Students, those from many other fields of study and some of my New City students attended the activities which happened in Drexel University classrooms, at the Drexel Armory, and at other locations in Philadelphia at no charge. Futurists and thinkers came from all over the United States and interacted with each other. Students brought models of their cities of the future. All my "NOs!" turned into "YESSES!"

After receiving my master's degree from the University of Colorado in Boulder in 1977, I taught the same class myself, twice, in the Adult Evening Program of St. Louis University. There my students included Police Officers, Housewives, businesspeople, and students from a variety of the University's Day programs. The word spread and the class size doubled the second time it was offered. Looking back, this class and the 2020 future's conference was to be the precursor for my global work with Interfaith.

What We Succeed At Creates the Foundation For More Success

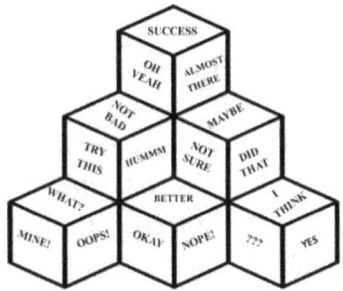

IF
ONLY
THINGS
WERE
DIFFERENT!

I Wish I Had!

Have you ever uttered the words, "I wish I had…"? Of course you have; everyone has. I wish I had travelled more. I wish I had married my childhood sweetheart. I wish I had gone into the work I love and not taken this job for the money. I wish I had done better in school. I wish I had stayed away from *that* person. I wish I had kept a better diet, maybe I'd be healthier. On and on there are always things that we may have wished for but did not activate our "doing" muscles to make happen. It could have been as small as I wish I hadn't eaten that fifth donut or those extra slices of pizza. We kick ourselves for not doing what our gut told us was right to do. And yet… the choices we made or didn't make, took us on a journey which has led us to where we are today.

In my 2004 book "**REBOOT**" which I wrote after suffering a stroke which paralyzed the left side of my body, I used the title as an acronym. Each letter stood for and still stands for a different phase of the REBOOTING process which we all go through when a change happens in our life. The first letter "R" stands for

**R = Realize You Have Changed
and You Can <u>Never</u> Be The Same**

(I'll discuss the other letters later in this book.)

Ignore the "No!"

This fact happens with everything we learn throughout our lifetime. Once you learn something, it is difficult to unlearn those facts. If you have learned and believe that one and one are two, it would be difficult for me to make you believe it is a different answer. If we burn our finger while trying to light a candle, we are much more aware of how not to get burned in the future. Someone who has hit their finger while driving a nail into a wood board, is much more careful the next time he or she wields a hammer. Anyone who has burned the family dinner once, will be more cautious the next time they are cooking. After we have made a mistake once, our brain sets up an alarm system to warn us when we are getting close to making the same mistake again. This is both good and bad.

The good part is that we will probably no longer burn our finger, hit our hand with a hammer, or overcook a meal. The bad point MAY BE that, due to our fear of failure, we may never even try to light another candle, or use a hammer or try to cook a meal. In our mind, the mistake may have become so blown out of proportion that we shy away from engaging in similar life activities. We are afraid to accept love from another because we have "lost at love" sometime in the past. We are afraid to consider investing our money because we were "swindled" once before. We are afraid to make a doctor appointment because we received a "bad diagnosis" once in the past which scared us. These fears and an infinite number more are all related to our brain hearing the word "NO!" and causing it to limit our future options and activities.

What if the love we are being offered now is from a true "soul partner" who wants the two of you to be happy together? What if through a legitimate company, with a small investment, there could be the possibility of a large financial return? What if by seeing the result of one doctor's test, your life could be lengthened or made better? What if ignoring the word "NO!" could actually bring you a better life?

"Chutzpah"

What I have learned over the years is that the word "NO!" is a barrier only to those who do not have a clear vision of or feel a real purpose for what they want. They do not have the faith that all things are possible.

Two bible passages have come to rule my life when it comes to creating my future. They are:

"According to your faith it will be done unto you." *Matthew: 9:29.*

"You have not because you ask not." *James: 4:2.*

The Hebrew word "Chutzpah" is an ideal word to use when planning something which we cannot fully articulate to others or even are clear about in our own mind. It is having the nerve to ask for something without any idea about how it may come to pass. I call it the "**Santa Trust Factor.**" We reluctantly affirm and ask for what we want with no idea how we are actually going to receive it.

Understanding two other concepts have also become a way of life for me – The concept that 'Energy Cannot be Created nor Destroyed' and that 'Everything is Energy.'

The simplest example we can use to understand the first is that of heating a pot of ice cubes. The amount of "energy" in the ice cubes can be seen, felt and easily weighed. As you begin to heat the pot, the ice turns to water. There is still exactly the same amount of energy in the water as there was in the ice cubes. THERE HAS TO BE! But it is in a different form.

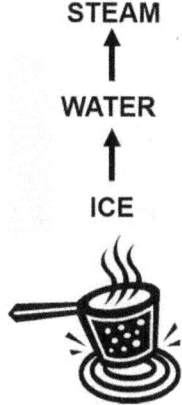

As we continue to heat the water it turns to steam. The energy in the steam is the same amount of energy that was in the water and was in the ice cubes. It is just in a different form. Whether in a solid form, a liquid or steam, the amount of energy MUST always be the same. Understanding this helps us to better understand many of the other things that happen to us and the other people around us during our lifetime.

The second concept has been scientifically proven over and over again and is even the premise of how our universe became what it is. The energy in the "Big Bang" explosion whether you believe God caused it to happen or not, has propelled substances from the "beginning" into what we can now measure and understand today; and it will continue to change into what will be the future of our universe. This concept also explains human death, transforming from a physical form to a spiritual form and helps us to realize how little we know despite our perceived advance technology. Scientists have proven that the elements of the energy which existed at the "Big Bang," now exists within every human life force in the world today.

So how does that relate to how we process the word "NO!"?

The word "NO!" like the word "YES!" when thought about and/or said orally, has energy. It is that energy which we formulate within ourselves, or outwardly, by using those and other words. The positive or negative words can help us propel towards a goal or to try, or not try, new things. Note: WE CAN DESCIDE WHICH WORD TO USE AT ANY MOMENT IN OUR LIFE! IT IS <u>ALWAYS</u> OUR CHOICE!

"Why Me Lord?"

The 3 words, "Why Me Lord?" are words which most spiritual human beings have verbally expressed at some time in their life. That can be a good or bad thing! It all depends on what we do AFTER we say those 3 words.

On April 13, 2003, I was in the hospital emergency room complaining about a severe pain in my neck and shoulder. At about 3pm with my wife looking on, I began to slur my words. Abigail called the doctor over and she confirmed that I was having a stroke at that moment. The left side of my body became paralyzed. It did not affect my cognitive functions. I could think and respond to the doctors and nurses and to my wife with a slurred speech, but I could not move any muscles on the left side of my body. This began my understanding of how a person REBOOTs a portion of his or her life.

I remember lying in my hospital bed a few hours later asking myself those 3 words. "Why me Lord? I'm a pretty good person. I'm a minister and I spend time helping others around me. Why ME Lord?"

Now I'm not sure whether any of us expects a booming voice to shout from the heavens and answer us at the moment when we utter those 3 words. The one thing I WAS SURE OF was, that at that moment, I would not like ANY of the answers I might receive. I knew it would be equal to hearing the word, "NO!" and I could not do anything about it!

"NO!" the stroke said, you have no choice! "NO!" half of your power to move has been taken away! "NO!" you have to lie there and there is nothing you can do about it. "NO!" Just because there has never been a stroke in your family, doesn't mean you can't have one now. "NO!" the fact that you are a minister and a good person, has no bearing as to what you are going through and what the weeks and months and years ahead will bring. "NO!" "NO!" "NO!"

Between the tears and the fears, I came to realize that I was not going to die. The tests showed that the clot which caused my stroke had passed and the only thing left to do was go into rehab. And this is where a major story for this book begins.

ATTITUDE

Makes a Difference

Two days after the stroke hit and I was found to be stable, and I was transferred in the afternoon to the St. Judes' Rehab hospital in Fullerton, CA for what was to be 4-6 weeks of intensive rehab care. I was thankful for carpeted hallways and the elimination of noisy medical carts racing quickly down the hall. I wasn't sure what they were going to do for me, but I was anxious to learn.

The first person I met the next morning was an Occupational Therapist who helped me dress and get ready for the day. As she evaluated my movements, I realized how little I could do without the muscles on the left side of my body. She showed me that if I take care of my weak side first, my strong side will take care of itself. This became a major rule for me to use later when counseling others.

I was taught coping skills to offset the paralysis such as when I brushed my teeth. Rather than "NO!" you cannot squeeze the toothpaste onto the toothbrush with your left hand, it was "YES" I could squeeze toothpaste into my mouth with my right hand and then use the toothbrush. I was learning all the "YES" techniques.

My "YES!" attitude came out strong with my next visitor. Rick was a large man and he was to be my primary Physical Therapist for the duration. I was fully dressed and sitting in a wheelchair as he entered my room to evaluate me. He slowly approached me staring only at my face. (As he got about a foot away from my face, I thought he was going to kiss me). Then Rick said something very factually, "You've had a stroke!" *I was happy to hear that he had read my chart!*

And then he continued talking, still staring at my face, "And there is a 10% chance that you will have another one." I stared at him and said with my garbled voice pattern, "Then there is a 90% chance that I will never have another stroke." Still staring at me, Rick took a few steps back and said, "You're Right! "For 15 years I have been telling stroke patients that fact and what you said to me is actually truer. You have just changed the way I will be talking with new stroke patients in the future." Hearing him say that I thought to myself, "THANK YOU GOD!" And the REBOOTING process began.

Rebooting To "Yes!"

When we go through a severe illness, or a messy divorce, or we have to declare bankruptcy, or we get fired from a job which we expected to retire in, dealing with all the "NO!" feedbacks can cause us to be very cynical about the world. The doctors told me that as healed as my body would become in six months of rehab, was all I could expect as far as a full recovery. To me that was another "NO!"

I refused to remain in the physical condition I came in with after the stroke and I continued to work hard beyond what was asked of me. When Rick or any of the other therapists would ask me to walk halfway down the hall, I always said, "No, let's go all the way down the hall." That brought out more "YES!" remarks no matter who I was working with. And whenever I could add humor and make people laugh, I found a way to do it.

One afternoon I found myself making cookies FROM SCRATCH in the hospital kitchen with another stroke patient. I couldn't use my left side and he couldn't use his right. So together we stirred in flour, eggs, butter, cinnamon, chocolate chips, nuts and as we did, the therapists roared and laughed during the entire routine of the two stroke patients making cookies. Not all of the ingredients stayed in the mixing bowls, but we created a 3-Stooge routine with just the two of us. P.S. The cookies were not all round, but they tasted great!

I healed more quickly than the doctor's expectations and later that year Abigail and I moved to a single-story home in Poway California. In 2004 after 13 months of healing, I began volunteering once a week at the Palomar Rehab Institute in Escondido, California.

My speech had come back to almost normal and because of my rehab experience, patients seemed to relate to me sometimes beyond how they related to the doctors, therapists and nurses around them. My nickname became "Tuesday Steve" as I always announced loudly that "IT'S TUESDAY" as I arrived on the hospital floor for my volunteer time. At times I did filing or made calls to patients who had gone home to find out how they were doing. My greatest gift was to be able to speak to patients who had recently had a stroke.

I remember Al. He was a husky man in his mid-forties, sitting in a wheelchair next to his bed when I walked into his hospital room. Looking very solemn and distrustful, he had had a similar stroke to what I had experienced and was NOT a happy camper. He was in "NO!" mode and in his mind expected to be sitting in that wheelchair for the rest of his life.

My opening line to him and to every rehab patient I first met, especially those who were there due to a stroke was, "Hi Al, I hear we have a lot in common." Al looked at me in total disbelief. Didn't I understand what he had been through? You are walking and talking and obviously healthy; how could you understand how angry and scared I am. As with every stroke and rehab patient I have ever met in the sixteen years I volunteered, up until the COVID-19 pandemic stopped visitations, I followed my first hello by telling him or her about my stroke and rehab. history. I garbled my words to resemble what I sounded like during the first six months after my stroke. Al sat there speechless with tears in his eyes. I told him that he should do what the therapists tell him and that he would start to see improvement. Then I left saying that I would see him next week.

A week later I walked into Al's room. He was sitting in his wheelchair in the same position I had left him in a week earlier. All I got to say was, "Hi Al." And then in a slow garbled stroke voice Al began to speak.

"When you came into my room last week, I knew what I had to do. I was going to kill myself. I have a gun in a drawer next to my bed at home and I did not want to live like this forever. And then you showed me that I could get better. And I am not going to kill myself now." Tears filled my eyes and all I could think in my head was, "Thank You God." I had gone through my stroke for this moment (and for hundreds of other similar moments thereafter).

All my "NOs!" All my asking "Why Me Lord?" All my fears and struggles, all my not being able to see the future clearly, all the uncertainty brought me to a place where I could ignore the NOs! Where my answer to "Why Me?" was, WHY NOT ME? And to the uncertainty in my future, it became a plan for me to decide, what did <u>I</u> want? So, I ask you, WHAT DO <u>YOU</u> WANT?

Your Future

What were your visions for your life as an adolescent? The wanting to ride on a fire engine or be a super-hero may have passed. The need to fit in with our friends became less important now, and we had to think about the possibilities for our own future. And hopefully by then we had learned, or are learning now, that our belief in the possibilities that are available for our life are limited only by that which we tell ourselves.

In 1989 as my architectural career was about to end, unbeknownst to me, I was in Chicago finishing the design and opening of another retail chain store. Since I was having to remain in Chicago alone through the weekend, the wife of the Franchisee who I was designing the store for asked me if I would like to come to church with them. I told her that I did not go to church. Then she offered to buy me lunch afterwards. So I said yes.

Besides my architectural career, I was also a part-time motivational speaker. Having left the synagogue which I was brought up in because the Rabbi had said "NO!" to my learning about Kabbalah (the Mystical branch of Judaism), I forged my own way into spirituality by researching the many religions. I studied Edgar Cayce's life and readings and practiced what was at the time strange stuff like hypnosis, past-life regression, meditation, and visualization. I became ordained on-line in 1982 and performed a few weddings and even a memorial. I joined National Speaker's Association in 1982 and wrote my first book in 1986. On the side I lectured and saw clients who had past-life issues as well as personal and/or family problems which I counselled them on. I saw no need to belong to a church since I viewed most of them as quite biased.

That Sunday morning as I entered the New Thought/Unity Church of Oak Park I was greeted warmly. However, I was looking forward to not being impressed for an hour or so and to having a nice lunch afterwards. Rev. Richard Billings came to the platform and began to describe New Thought and UNITY. My mouth dropped open as he repeated words to the congregation which I had told my clients. He then led a meditation in keeping with my positive thinking and past-life regression techniques and I remember being stunned by the many similarities in the verbiage. The music was enjoyable and positive and was followed up with a sermon unlike any I had ever heard in a church. I thought to myself that he had read my book *(which he obviously had not)*.

After the service I approached Rev. Billings, introduced myself and in no uncertain terms asked, "WHAT IS THIS NEW THOUGHT/UNITY STUFF?" I said that what I had heard and what he had spoken about is what I had been teaching for the last twenty years. He gave me some New Thought/Unity literature to read and, hearing that I was in town for business, asked me where I called home. When I told him San Diego, he invited me to look up Rev. Wendy Craig-Purcell and visit her church one Sunday. He also asked that I consider coming back to Chicago and speaking at his church one Sunday. I was too confused at the moment to say "YES" but I left without a "NO!" On the plane ride home, I devoured the Unity material and six months later I was his guest speaker and then again, six months after that.

YOUR FUTURE MAY BE BEYOND YOUR PRESENT COMPREHENSION

You can't see where you are going? Your future is not clear? What are you ASKING for? Are you ASKING for CLARITY? You see...if in your daily prayer work instead of "asking for clarity" you are "BEGGING for STUFF" such as a new love or a new job or more money or better health, **then you are misdirecting your energy**! Begging for stuff, emphasizes (in your mind) that you don't have which you need or want now. It is like telling yourself that you have failed. It is a BIG "NO!" And you created it.

By ASKING FOR CLARITY, you are not limiting yourself to what you think you deserve. Perhaps you believe that you deserve a certain yearly salary; however, would you be open to receiving more than that? Would you be open to not just curing your perceived illness but making your entire body healthy?

And what about your career? The end of the Chicago story for me was that when I returned to San Diego, the President of the company told me that they would be going out of business over the next two months and that my architectural design position would no longer be needed. And, within two weeks of returning home I attended Rev. Wendy Craig-Purcell's Unity Church and was there until I met my future wife in 1999. Abigail, who became ordained as a New Thought minister in a sister New Thought church and I, opened our own New Thought church in 2000. We're still together!

"NO!" WHEN YOUR GUT SAYS "YES"

On February 17, 2012, I was doing my morning mile walk around the neighborhood and I experienced symptoms of a shortness of breath. When I got home, I quickly called my cariologist for an appointment and got to see him that afternoon. I told him "Something is wrong" and after his examination he told me "NO!" and that EVERYTHING was fine. I told him "NO!" I am not fine and that I want a stress test. He said "NO!" you do not need a stress test" and that his examination proved I was fine. I said "NO!" I am not fine, and I want a stress test." He said it was a waste of time but that I should speak to the scheduling nurse on the way out.

Luckily, I had become friends with the scheduling nurse, and she believed my plea for the earliest stress test appointment. I was back in the office at 10:00 the next morning. The nurse had me all wired up for the treadmill test when the cardiologist came in physically displaying that this procedure was a waste of his time. 30 seconds after starting the treadmill stress test he ended the session and he scheduled an angiogram for me that afternoon at the local hospital. The doctor completed the angiogram and white-faced, told my wife in the waiting room that all of my heart arteries were blocked up to 90% and that I would need open heart surgery. The 5-way bypass open heart surgery was performed 2 days later by a more than competent group of doctors and I obviously survived.

When your gut tells you something LISTEN!

Oh, it's just my imagination. I'm making a mountain out of a molehill. It'll go away in a little while. These and other evasive beliefs may be the difference between life and death. <u>YOUR LIFE OR DEATH</u>! Unless you are using mind-altering drugs, your "feelings" need to be listened to and given credence. Had I not insisted that I needed to have that stress test, I know that I would have died soon after.

Each of us was born into this world with a set of purposes. Those purposes are usually not apparent until we are fulfilling them. After the heart operation, I was told that "NO!" I could not volunteer at the rehab hospital for 6 weeks. By then everything would have healed enough, and I should have much of my strength back. But after 4 weeks, something was driving me to go back to the hospital for a visit and to thank my rehab friends whose care I was under for the last few days after my operation.

I walked onto the rehab floor of Palomar hospital, and announced that "IT"S TUESDAY!" I was immediately warmly welcomed by the therapists and nurses who had been my friends for eight years. My good friend, Dr. Keyvan Esmaeili, who ran the rehab institute and who everyone called "Dr. Smiley" because he smiled so much, greeted me with a big smile and a loose hug. He said, "You're not supposed to be back here yet" for which I replied, "It's good to see you too." After exchanging "how are you feeling" news, I asked Dr. Smiley how things were going. I could see in his face that there was a problem and I said, "What's Up?"

He told me that we had a Russian rehab patient, in his late sixties, who had just come out of open-heart surgery. He was in the normal pain after such an operation, but he was VERY depressed. The worst part was that he did not speak English. His adult son stayed at the hospital as much as he could to be able to translate between his father and the medical staff. Dr. Smiley asked me if I wanted to visit him and "do my magic" but not to expect anything. I certainly did not speak Russian and I was not sure if I could be of any help. But I took it as another possible "NO!" and went to his room anyway.

When I stood in the doorway of his room, a nurse was just completing the rebandaging of the patient's chest. I remembered the procedure well. The patient's son was seated in a chair to the right side of the bed and he and his father looked at me in a manner that said, "What do YOU want?"

I do not know what inspired me. All of a sudden, I found myself lifting up my rehab polo shirt and exposing my bare chest with all the many marks from my open-heart surgery. The son immediately stood up and smiled. The patient looked at his son in a "What is this" manner and I looked at the patient and told the son that I had the same operation 4 weeks before. The son told that to his father and the patient smiled. We were now family. Over the next 10-15 minutes we discussed our surgeries via his son and the fact that I had bragging rights because he had a 3-way bypass, while I had had a FIVE-way bypass! We laughed while comparing our illnesses. When I left, the patient was smiling and understood that he was in the best place to get well and that the doctors and nurses were very competent to help him do that.

God Uses Us For Good

Dr. Smiley and I talked about it afterwards saying that it was no coincidence that I had stopped by that morning. No one else on the hospital staff could have had the positive effect that came from my surprise visit. Whatever negativity has happened in our life, using it as a positive teaching tool for others to make their bad event a good thing, helps the healing process in all who are affected. And it isn't until you experience someone else receiving "good" from your past problem, that you can recognize the reward.

An Unexpected "No!"

In mid-March of 2012, I was at a Sikh temple celebrating the Sikh New Years. A Sikh friend of mine who had heard about my open-heart surgery, came over to ask how I was doing and that they had been praying for me. Thanking him, I offered my congratulations on the Sikh New Year and he asked me, "When is the New Thought New Year?" I looked at Abigail, thought for a moment and replied, "We do not have one" and "This is a no-brainer."

Unlike Christianity which has almost 41,000 different religious denominations and many different ways of experiencing the religion, in 2012 New Thought only had twelve branches. The funny thing was that all twelve taught almost the exact same thing. In general, they used the same books, quoted from the same authors, and sang many of the same songs. In Islam there are at least 5 major sects, in Judaism there are 4 major branches. Buddhism counts 3 major denominations and in the Pagan Religions there are over 30 distinct witch types. However, all of the different faiths had a yearly New Year's celebration except New Thought. So, I had a new goal; I would create a yearly holiday for all of New Thought. It would be one day a year to remember our history.

"New Thought, not to be confused with New Age, is more than a century-old, practically oriented spiritual faith which promotes fullness of all aspects of living. It embraces positive thinking, listening to one's inner voice, affirmative prayer, meditation, and other ways of realizing the presence of God within. It began in the mid-1800s with Ralph Waldo Emerson and Phineas P. Quimby who both came to believe the mind can create good health or it can create disease." Ernest Holmes explained that "The philosophy of Religious Science/ New Thought is nothing new to the world. It is rather a synthesis of the greatest concepts that have ever come to the mind of humankind. The laws of Moses, the love of Christ, the ethics of Buddha, the morals of Confucius and the deep spiritual realization of the Hindus all find an exalted place in the philosophy of Religious Science/New Thought." (The Interfaith Manual, 2008, Albert)

I did my research and began a PowerPoint presentation about the beginnings and growth of New Thought. Then I contacted a few of my New Thought colleagues and heard, "NO!" "NO!" "NO!" "NO!" "It's a great idea but it can't be done." "There's too much politics & egos involved."

Is This Starting to Sound Familiar?

I spoke to colleagues in most of the different New Thought branches and they told me the same thing. "NO!" "NO!" "NO!" "NO, It Can't be done!" So, I questioned myself and backed down reluctantly.

In 2012, Abigail and I belonged to the Association of New Thought Network (ANTN) which was one of the 12 branches of New Thought. Abigail was the President that year and I was scheduled to be a guest speaker during their annual conference in Scottsdale, Arizona. The executive director at the time was Rev. Kim Yalda who preceded my presentation with a PowerPoint history of New Thought. It was the perfect compilation of what I had begun a few months earlier. I saw it as a sign that the universe was telling me that a New Thought holiday was possible. I asked Kim if I could integrate her presentation into the one I was developing and she said, "Of course." Yet, even with that reassurance, when I spoke with other New Thought ministers who attended the conference, all I got was "NO! it can't be done! Getting all the branches of New Thought to agree on anything, was not going to happen."

The Universe Says "YES" When Others Close The Door!

Two months later, Abigail and I were in Rome, Italy for the Association of Global New Thought's Awakened World's Conference. We both were facilitators of daily discussion groups whose members came from various faiths and religions in the world. At the first night's dinner, we found ourselves sitting across from Rev. Dr. Kenn Gordon who was the Spiritual Director of Centers for Spiritual Living which was another New Thought branch. Since I had nothing to lose and I was talking to one of the "biggies," I posed the question of "what is your opinion about creating a yearly New Thought holiday?" Stunned, I heard him quickly say, "That's a great idea; I'd vote for that."

HE DIDN'T SAY "NO!"

A few months later in 2013, after having spoken directly to each of the leaders of the New Thought branches individually and having gotten a "YES" from each, New Thought Day became a reality happening on the first Sunday of March every year. The Interfaith Marketplace listed it on its Multifaith Calendar which they send out to the world every year. Another "NO!" had become a "YES."

Let's Be Honest

The facts are that if you are under 5 feet tall, you probably will never be on a professional basketball team. SO WHAT! That doesn't mean you cannot watch and enjoy the game!

What do you love to do? And what would you like to do? What excites your interest? IF IT WAS NOT IMPOSSIBLE, what would you like to accomplish? This is the mindset and overall message this book advocates. It does not matter how many "NO!" responses you have received in the past. It does not matter how many times you failed, and it does not matter what others think about you.

If you are still skeptical, try this experiment. Walk down a busy street and look at people who are passing you by. Try to imagine what each of those people are thinking, what do they do for a living, if they are married, how many kids do they have and what mistakes did they make during the past week. Now continue walking and try to remember which person did what. Within minutes you will give up thinking about them because... <u>You Really Don't Care About Them</u>! And you know what, they don't care about you either! They don't care what you are wearing, if you have a stain on your shirt or pants, if you have your makeup on, if your hair is blonde or pink, or whether you wear jockeys or briefs. Nobody cares about you. Well, there may be some family members who do. Parents, spouse, children and close friends probably wish the best for you, but OTHERS DON'T CARE!

With almost 8 billion people on this planet, you can probably count on one hand those who are not too busy with their own life to think about you in any depth. They think, "I wonder how what's his name is doing?" and then they continue to decide what they are going to prepare for dinner.

So, if no one is watching you and no one cares about you anyway, why not try to do something wonderful, something others view as impossible? You cannot fail. You don't have to climb Mount Everest (unless you want to), you don't have to try out for the Olympic team (unless you want to), and you do not have to put yourself in any danger. People around the world have accomplished wonderful things and commented later that, "I never thought I would be doing this!" They smile at their accomplishments and are thanked by others whose names they may never know.

In the May 20, 2022, Reader's Digest, there was a listing of non-famous, ordinary people who changed history. Rosa Parks would not give up her seat on the bus; Todd Beamer and the passengers of Flight 93 fought back against 9/11 terrorists who took over their plane, Candy Lightner stood up against drunk driving and made a difference in the law. And I love the picture of the single Chinese man who stood directly in front of a military tank near Tiananmen Square in China to protest the war. What are you willing to stand up for?

Goals Change Over Time

In 2004 Abigail saw an ad in a local Poway paper announcing that members of the Baha'i Faith were organizing an Interfaith Peace conference and were inviting people of different faiths to join them in planning the one-day event. Neither Abigail nor I knew what a Baha'i was, so we joined them one evening at a local restaurant. Abigail became one of the faith speakers explaining the New Thought faith to the community along with six other speakers from different faiths. After the second year, the speakers suggested that they should continue meeting. Together in 2005 they became the founding members of the Poway Interfaith Team whose goal was to educate the public about various faith traditions. **No one** said, "NO!"

Ignore the "NO!"

Abigail and I still remained the co-ministers of our New Thought center teaching New Thought beliefs and yet, our hearts kept being drawn into the Interfaith group and the work it was doing in the community to bring together people of different faiths.

In 2008, Abigail and I attended our first ANTN Connect conference in San Francisco. At that point we still believed that we were among the minority of groups in the country doing interfaith work. At the 3-day conference we met nearly 100 people from all over the United States, Canada and Mexico who were doing the same work. We were inspired to go back to Poway and increase our involvement with Interfaith. One other major thing happened at the San Francisco conference. We were told about the Parliament of World's Religions (PWR) conference which happened every 3-5 years. It was going to happen in Melbourne Australia the next year and we were told, "YOU CANNOT MISS IT!"

In 2009, we travelled to Melbourne Australia, which was another location on our Vision Board, and were overwhelmed by the 8,000 people from 80 different countries who attended the 5-day session and who were involved with Interfaith work in their area of the world. Christians and Muslims, Buddhists and Jews, and people from over 80 different faiths intermingled as friends and we were hooked! Our focus went from strictly New Thought to Interfaith and how to share our beliefs with others and learn more about their beliefs.

Over the years POINT, as it came to be called, has grown to represent 18 different faith groups plus individual members and to have an excellent reputation for creating peaceful involvement between people from various faiths and professions. We became so effective and had so many connections in San Diego, that we were invited to host a 3-1/2 day "Connect Conference" in 2017 for the North American Interfaith Network. That's when all the "NO!" comments began to show up again. "NO!" as to where to hold the conference, "NO!" as to what colors the logos and flyers should have, "NO!" about which foods and snacks to offer, and on and on and on. The one thing we all agreed on was, due to the abundance of Interfaith talent we had in San Diego, we would need at least one extra day of activities to fit them all in. NAIN had never been asked to extend their Connect conference before and we were told by their planning board that "NO!" it cannot be done. We went to their board of Directors and showed them the preliminary program and they finally gave us the "YES!"

For 4-1/2 days during the second week in August in 2017 at the University of California San Diego, we hosted 77 speakers, workshops, meditations, parties, bus trips to historic faith locations, an ice cream social, and extensive interfaith dialogue with over 250 people. We wanted to get the surrounding cities involved but we were told by many people "NO!" it will never happen. "NO! you won't be able to do get politicians involved with faith-related subjects."

Months before the event, we contacted all the City Mayors in San Diego County and the County itself and asked them and their city council to issue a proclamation for the conference and Interfaith Awareness Week. The proclamation read, *"We honor and respect all faiths, cultures, creeds, and races and seek to learn from those who believe equal spiritual opportunity and human rights belong to every person."* This has become the mission statement for the World Interfaith Network which I created in 2020 and now direct world-wide. I had come to live by *"You Have Not because You Ask Not"* so I asked. 14 City Mayors and City Councils in San Diego County, as well as the County supervisors themselves, agreed and issued a proclamation for the event

What do you need to ask for in your life? How might you positively change someone's life by your words, actions or deeds? Perhaps those people who <u>should</u> know something, do not. Perhaps at some unconscious level, they are waiting for you to enlighten them. You might change their "NO!" to "YES!"

Interfaith Awareness Week which I direct, has become a Global celebration put on by the World Interfaith Network since 2018. In 2022, we put on a 7-day, 12-hours-a-day virtual conference which united interfaith groups and people from throughout the United States, Canada, Mexico, Brazil, England, Australia, Pakistan, and Israel. Miracles can happen when you learn to Ignore the "NO!"

Speaking About Miracles

The "M" word is something which many people find hard to accept or discuss. Webster defines it as "an extraordinary event <u>manifesting</u> divine intervention in human affairs; an extremely outstanding or unusual event, thing, or accomplishment; a divinely natural phenomenon experienced humanly as the fulfillment of spiritual law." The reason people find a miracle hard to accept is because they cannot logically understand the details of it and how it could come about.

Remember when we were growing up. There was so much to learn. Most of the adults in our lives accepted that our learning to read and write was just part of that growing process. I look at my 2-year-old granddaughter and I am amazed at how much she understands and reacts to in the short time she has been on Earth. The fact that she is even alive is a miracle to me. Of course, I intellectually understand how a child is conceived, grows, is born and nurtured. He or she learns from all that which is in their surroundings. But with all my 75 years of trying to understand how things work in this world, most of what I know about I still consider a miracle.

The fact that I accomplished so much after my high school counselor told me I wasn't college material, was that a miracle? The fact that I created a Faith's yearly holiday after being told by colleagues that it couldn't be done, was that a miracle? Is the fact that I didn't die from my stroke or 5-way bypass, open-heart surgery, were those miracles too?

Take a deep breath, is your breathing a miracle? Having 60,000 miles of blood vessels in your body circulating the needed blood and nutrients to all your organs and throughout your body, is that a miracle? When you do a crossword puzzle or someone asks you a question AND YOU ANSWER THEM CORRECTLY, is that a miracle? If all this and much more is happening without your needing to really think about it, would you consider that you might be able to do the impossible when someone tells you "NO!"?

What if the answer was always "YES"?

As strange as it sounds, have you ever imagined your life if you were never to hear the word "NO!" again? What if all the negativity and the upset in your life changed and were replaced with what you want? What if everything you tried for happened easily? What would that look like? WHAT WOULD YOU ACTUALLY WANT?

Preparing for "YES" is as important as receiving it. This is exactly what many people who play the lottery wish for but have not fully envisioned. The funny thing is that 70% of people who win a large sum of money in the lottery, are poor again within a few years. Why? Because being "rich" is not about money; it is about consciousness. Most people who hope to never hear the word "NO!" again, have not planned for a life where everything is "YES!" It is like the trick-or-treater who wakes up the morning after Halloween with a bellyache because he ate all his candy the night before. He didn't consider all the possible things which might go wrong.

IGNORE THE "NO!"

So, the question really is, if you didn't have any "NO!" in your life, what would you do with all the Yesses?

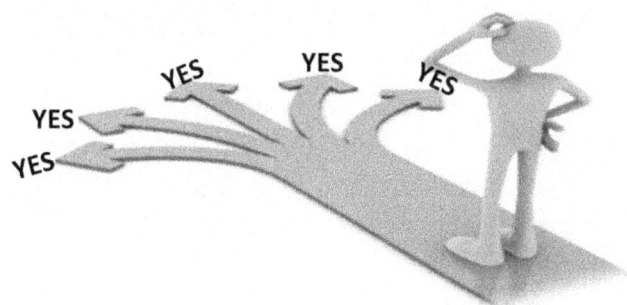

The Use of Previous Thought

Planning for what you want to receive takes practice. Yes, you can have it all. Now think about what that would look like and how you would maneuver through your day if you had it all. Imagine yourself waking up in the morning. What is your plan for the day? Use the bathroom, wash your face and brush your teeth? You can do that because you *previously* bought toilet paper, soap, toothpaste, and a toothbrush. You have a clean towel to dry yourself with because you *previously* did the laundry and washed your towels. You move to the kitchen to prepare your morning coffee and have breakfast. That is easily done because you *previously* went shopping and bought coffee, eggs, bread, butter and even a sweet role to treat yourself with. Your entire day depends upon what you have *previously* done. Want to use the car to go to work, shopping, or to visit friends? You can do that, IF you *previously* remembered to fill the car's tank with gas.

Without "previous thought," all the easy Yesses cannot exist. So, what if we begin to pre-schedule all of the "previous thought" so as to help us avoid future "NOs!" This is where visioning and meditation becomes essential. Typically, if you were to go shopping for new clothes, you might not know what you should buy? If you need a dress, suit, shirt or a tie for a "particular" event, choosing the right garment becomes much easier.

It is harder to shop for something if you do not know how you might use it or what the occasion might be. The same is true about life. If you do not consider how to get to where you want to go, there is a greater possibility of you getting lost.

Ignore the "No!"

Creating a Vision Board (VB) is an ideal way to help you focus in on the details of what you believe you want in life. I've had one for over 20 years. Some people like to have their VB mounted on a wall somewhere in their home or office. I prefer to create a smaller VB which I can easily carry with me on vacations or business trips. Mine is in a 8-1/2" by 11" plastic sleeve and is 3-hole punched for access to fit into my day planner. The fun part of creating a VB is that we can scan through magazines and brochures and cut out pictures to paste onto our VB. We can choose pictures of where we want to travel, the kind of job we would like to have, and we can make a list of the characteristics we prefer to have in a new romantic partner if that is what we desire. All of this allows us to graphically visualize the type of life we want to create.

I didn't know it at the time but, all the house designs I was creating in high school for my drafting class, were developing in my mind the process of architecturally designing spaces in the future. The high school drawings were obviously not professional but as a sixteen-year-old, I could envision how I wanted the rooms to be laid out and how circulation would occur.

I remember having on my VB beautiful pictures of Hawaii which, it turns out many years later, was where Abigail and I were married. And Australia was on our VB which we connected to at the PWR. I had, and still have on my VB, one picture of a crowded auditorium with attendees seated looking at a large screen at the front of the room. I added a picture of me onto the screen and I envisioned me speaking to crowds of people. Under the picture I wrote, "I AM Spiritually led to Teach and Motivate others toward their Highest Good." I am happy to say, that vision has manifested in reality more times than I can count.

SEE yourself in detail doing what you want to do! You don't have to know HOW it will happen, but you are creating the *"Previous Thoughts"* which you will look back on when those things do manifest in your life. ENVISION the impossible and watch it come true for you.

Rev. Dr. Stephen Albert

When I created the World Interfaith Network (WIN) website, I wanted it to be a database for anyone looking for an interfaith group to join. When you visit https://world-interfaith.com online, you will see that there are almost 300 groups listed throughout the United States, Canada and other parts of the world. But I also wanted to create a fun atmosphere for people who went to the website, especially when we were in the midst of leading a global conference as we did during Interfaith Awareness Week in August of 2022.

Since the COVID epidemic curtailed people from meeting in person at the time, I wanted to bring people together virtually for fun. I still believe that meeting in person is the ideal way to create friendships and future joint activities. The not-being-able to have a cup of coffee together let alone a meal, really bothered me. I wanted to be able for visitors to the website to share VIRTUAL food and then joke about it being Sugar-free, Calorie-free, Gluten-free, Kosher and Halal. So, I asked my Techie friends, "Can we create a Virtual Interfaith Café? They said, "NO!" "It can't be done."

I visioned it! In my mind I SAW people enjoying a Virtual meal together and laughing about it during one of the conference sessions. **After all these years, the word "NO!" and the limiting meaning behind it, was no longer an option for me!** The more times we convert "NO!" to "YES!", the easier it is to bring future dreams into reality. After months of "NO!" replies, one techie friend of mine combined 3 different computer programs and the WIN Interfaith Café became a reality. You can enjoy a meal yourself when you go to the WIN website. *[Watch out for the glazed cinnamon buns; they are habit forming].*

We can take the visioning one step deeper when we combine it with daily meditation. If you have never meditated, learn how and start now.

MEDITATION

Do you ever daydream? Do you ever stare into space and just let your thoughts carry you to other places? Have you ever imagined yourself living a different type of life or perhaps living in a different country? How many secret fantasies have you locked up in your mind which you have never shared. Many people ignore those fantasies believing they are impossible.

Do you remember being a child in grade school? As we sat at our desk, we stared out the window to discover some revolutionary concept or to project our self to some fun-filled land. In a flash we would be flying in a plane or perhaps in free flight across the sky. The slightest key word, change in the weather, or even a smell in the air whisked us off to new adventures and new challenges. We had the power to change our physical body to be bigger or stronger. We gave ourselves the controls to be smarter, funnier, happier, or more inventive. Through our daydreams we could become anything we wished. And nobody said, "NO!"

Oh, Those Were The Days!

What about today? Do you still daydream, or have you suppressed the childlike quality of imagining? At times through peer pressure, we are dissuaded from exploring what could be, and we settle for what is. If you have heard "NO!" too much, that might be you.

If you do not daydream, it is probably not your fault. The controls which are placed on us when we are young can stifle free thinking. Perhaps in the middle of too many nice daydreams your teacher called your name to make you pay attention. She would say, "How do you ever expect to learn anything if you do not pay attention?" Parents may have demanded you "Pay attention if you want to get ahead in life." Friends may have made fun of you while you daydreamed past everyday life and got lost in tomorrow's possibilities.

If you do not daydream now, would you like to? Would you like to redevelop your creative power to expand what you know? Would you like to expand your mental capabilities to experiment with conceptual ideas and possibilities? Almost every invention on earth was developed by people who daydreamed. Would you like to invent something?

Daydreaming allows our mind to wander. It allows us to plan, set goals, and possibly come up with new ideas for our life. The only unfortunate aspect about daydreaming is it is a spontaneous occurrence and, therefore, can be difficult to use as a tool to help us plan to reach our goals.

Meditation is the closest PLANNED act we can perform which gives us the benefits of daydreaming and, at the same time allows us to communicate within. I do not like the word meditation. I prefer to call the act of Planned Daydreaming. For many people, the word meditation connotes strange and nonproductive behavior. Due to the myths about meditation, many adults will not allow themselves to look further into the subject. However, I do not know another word which can more completely describe a planned daydream state of mind.

People enjoy that portion of a fishing trip when they are alone and can allow their minds to relax and think of nothing. Busy men and women look for a place to "crash" so they can rid themselves of the day's stresses. Almost anyone you speak with, will admit they would like to find a way to stop and clear their minds of their daily responsibilities even if just for a little while. If we can just get rid of some of the fallacies the word has come to represent, meditation is a valid answer.

The fallacies are many. I find that, to reach a deeper and higher level of consciousness, we DO NOT have to sit in the lotus position. We do not have to wear certain types of clothing nor sit facing a particular direction. We do not have to burn incense or candles, and we do not have to be a vegetarian. Drinking herbal teas or avoiding sexual activity have nothing to do with meditation. There is no one way to meditate; and we do not have to belong to any special meditation groups to get the proper spiritual response.

Daydreaming, becoming one with ourselves, looking within, finding inner peace, praying, meditation, or whatever we want to call a planned session of personal quiet can be the most important thing we ever do for ourselves. This is our self-programming time when we develop personal goals and learn to vision and expand our abilities. This is the time when we solve problems and work out physical and/or mental challenges. In the meditative state we can go beyond space and time and all physical barriers. This is a time to love our self and say "YES!".

Isn't It Time We Gave More Love to Our Self?

In order to get maximum results when we first begin to meditate, there are only two stipulations we need to adhere to — do not meditate when tired, and do not meditate in a room full of distractions. Eventually we will be able to meditate at any time and in any place.

The reason not to meditate when we are tired is, simply, we will fall asleep. If we are relaxing our body and mind so we can program ourselves for goal setting, the last thing we want to do is to fall asleep. Finding a time early in the morning, at lunch, or before or after dinner gives us a chance to get to know ourselves better and to program our self for a good rest when we do want to fall asleep.

If you choose to meditate at home and there are other people in the house, tell them you need their help. Ask them to respect your needs for privacy and quiet for the short time you will be meditating. If total quiet does not occur, do not stress yourself. Relaxation comes from internal quiet first.

What is internal quiet? Have you ever tried to fall asleep, but your mind kept wandering from one subject to the next? How am I going to pay that car insurance bill? How will I tell my boss I want a raise? What shall I tell my parents about the new "special" friend in my life? This is NOT internal quiet. Internal quiet happens when you allow your mind to concentrate on only that which you want it to. Sometimes it can be difficult.

If you find yourself having difficulty reaching internal quiet, try the following. Before you close your eyes, write down on a pad of paper any major projects you are working on. They could be projects from work or home or from wherever. Be conscious of the fact that you cannot achieve internal quiet when you have major projects on your mind. By writing them down you give them importance and you can be assured you will not forget those items. They will be waiting for you when you finish your meditation. By doing this, you are mentally prioritizing your immediate life's projects and making way for internal quiet. You can also use the same process if you are having trouble falling asleep.

After you've found a comfortable place to sit or lie down, position yourself so one leg is not on top of another. This may cause a circulation problem you will have to attend to during your meditation. And now...RELAX!

REEEEELAXX

Close your eyes and tell yourself to RELAX.

By telling yourself to relax, your mind listens to your mental command and has no choice but to relax. Take a deep, cleansing breath; fill your lungs to full capacity. Breathe in through your nose and out through your mouth and know the air you are taking into your lungs is cleansing your body. Know your lungs and vital organs are receiving clean air which is necessary for their proper operation. Know each time you relax, your body regenerates itself and becomes healthier.

Mentally encircle your body with a white light of protection from God and know God is helping you to relax and is protecting you in all you do. Remember, God always says "YES!" if it is for your highest good.

Take a second deep breath and this time tell yourself "more and more relaxed." Allow your body to feel the relaxation coming into it. Inhale slowly and exhale at the same rate. This regulates your body's respiratory system and calms you even more. Now you are ready to begin the simplest relaxation program you will ever experience. There are no mysteries, no special incantations, no magic words, just the desire to become relaxed.

First, tell your feet to relax. Do not TRY to make them relax, just know they are relaxing. I remember my first attempt at meditation. I was paying too much attention to my body responding to the commands of "relax." My mind became preoccupied with the process, and I found I could not relax.

Feel the relaxation spread slowly upward from the soles of your feet through your ankles, into your calves, your knees, up into your thighs, into your buttocks, and then up to your waist. Know every muscle, tendon, and fiber of your body from your waist down is completely relaxed. Feel each portion of your body relaxing and allow the relaxation to massage any tired or sore muscles into relaxed and healthy muscles. YOU are in control of your body relaxing.

As the relaxation begins to spread upward from your waist, take another deep cleansing breath and feel your abdomen and all your inner organs relaxing. Feel your heart relax as you slowly release the air from your lungs and know your heart will work better because of this relaxation.

Allow the relaxation to move upward into your chest and shoulders and then down into each arm, through the biceps, the elbows, the forearms, the wrists, the hands, and into each finger of each hand. Know every muscle, tendon, and fiber of your body from the shoulders down is totally and completely relaxed.

Now allow the relaxation to spread upward from your shoulders into your neck, massaging your neck into total relaxation; into your jaw and face, relaxing all of your facial muscles; and then into your head so your entire body is completely and perfectly relaxed.

Feel a sense of total relaxation and remember it. Experience the pleasure of being in full relaxation and thank yourself for being there. When you first begin to meditate you may want to take five minutes or more getting to a full body relaxation. As you begin to get into a daily routine of meditation, you will eventually be able to reach this relaxed state in seconds.

What I do once my body has reached a full level of relaxation is to count backward from twenty to ten and to know my body is moving into a deeper and deeper level of relaxation with each descending number.

Count down: twenty...nineteen...eighteen...deeper and deeper, seventeen...sixteen...fifteen...more and more relaxed, fourteen...thirteen...twelve...eleven and ten.

At ten our body reaches what is called the Alpha Level of relaxation. If your body was hooked up to sensitive recording devices in a laboratory, scientists would say your brain is producing Alpha Rhythms. Now your mind has a chance to dream and program itself to do anything it needs or wants to do. This is the point where you can concentrate on your visions or solve problems which are bothering you. It is here you can attract all your "YESSES!" and consider new projects you might want to begin.

You can spend as much time as you like in this stage of relaxation and, when you are ready to awaken, you can begin to program your actions for when you will return to the conscious level. Affirm for yourself "I am handling all of my daily problems calmly" or "I am in total control of my anger or fear." You can tell yourself your night's sleep will be very relaxed, and you will awaken the next morning refreshed and reenergized for the day. The options are limitless.

A slow count from ten to twenty brings you back to the conscious level very easily. Know always you are in full control of your relaxation and, if necessary, you can reach the conscious state in a second if you need to.

So, let's count up; ten...eleven...twelve...feel your body getting stronger and stronger, thirteen...fourteen...fifteen...feel your body getting healthier and healthier, sixteen...seventeen...eighteen...your eyes are now beginning to open, nineteen...and twenty. You are now totally awake at the conscious level.

As we begin to expand our visioning skills, it is important to be proficient in some type of meditation so you can have peaceful control of your mental and emotional processes most of the time. Having control can mean the difference between a happy life and an exceptionally fulfilling one. The more times you meditate, become peaceful, and transfer control to your waking hours, the easier it is to explore and expand your other abilities. Did you notice that there were no "NOs!" in the process? You stifled the "NO!"

Meditation = Control = Happiness
Without any "NO!s"

When "NO!" is the Answer!

We have all heard the term, "You can't win them all." Just because we are unhappy with the results, doesn't mean the "NO!" is wrong. Sometimes, the universe says "NO!" because something better is about to appear for us or for someone else.

As children we see things that we want and we yell, "MINE!" But there are some things which are not supposed to be ours at the time and "NO!" is appropriate. I say "NO!" to my wonderful, adorable, "I'd-give-my-life-for," two-year-old granddaughter; I love you and "NO!" you cannot play with the antique crystal glass ornament.

And just because we are attracted to that new person in our workplace, does not mean that he or she has to be attracted to us. Ignoring "NO!" works when we do not tread on another person's desires in life. Remember, they deserve to have "YES!" in their life too.

Ask any person who got married very young in life and who had not really had a chance to "know" the other person which they later divorced. When a person remarries, they usually approach the union with much more understanding and mature eyes.

The more times we mature through experiencing a mistake we've made and receiving a "NO!", the more times we will get closer to the "YES!" for what is truly ours to have. Many times we do not even know where the "YES" will come from.

In 1981, I was designing stores for a chain of well-known Ice Cream parlors. I had been there for 18 months when the company hired a new Vice President who would oversee the work of my department. My boss. the chief Architect, told me to "watch out" for this guy who had come from a well-known fast-food chain and had a very disruptive reputation. One morning the new VP came into our department and peered over my shoulder to see what I was working on. He pointed to the front entrance of the store and commented that there was too much room between the entrance and the first counter. I told him that the extra space was for handicapped access. He told me "tighten it up!" I explained that the planning department for that city would not approve an entrance any smaller than the one I had drawn. He told me in no uncertain terms, "I'm the boss and I want you to shrink that entrance space."

After he left, my boss who had overheard what the VP said to me said, "we have to do what he says" and that "I should change the plans based on what he had demanded." Reluctantly I did, and less than a week later we received notice that the city's planning department would not approve the plans which did not meet handicapped access. When the Vice President heard that, he was livid and walked up to me at my desk and fired me. I received his actions as a BIG "NO!" even though I knew I had done nothing wrong.

I packed up my things after my boss told me that he was sorry about what had occurred, but he had no power to change the VP's actions. Angry, I left the building and, on the way home I stopped by to see a friend who was the President of a small chain of computer stores. I needed to vent, and he was a good listener. I told him what had happened, and I asked him to let me know if he hears of any openings I might apply for. His loud response was very unexpected:

"ARE YOU KIDDING ME?!!!"

He told me that his company had been in chapter 11 (reorganization) for a year and earlier THAT morning had received word that they were cleared to continue developing stores. TO THAT END... he was looking for a new store designer to redesign their company image and carry the development of the company forward world-wide. Both of us believed in nothing being a coincidence and we smiled at each other knowing this was to be.

Your ""NO!" in the morning might turn into a "YES!" in the afternoon.

Sometimes a "NO!" happens to propel us forward to where we need to be. I was with that computer company for almost five years and designed over 360 stores around the world for them. It was one of the major highlights of my design career.

Receiving a "NO!" from a university which you applied to, may propel you into the perfect school to help you develop your talents BEYOND what you thought you should be studying. I have heard from many people who attended a university to study one thing, and then changed their major halfway through their schooling. Their first choice ended up as a "NO!" Their later choice was a "YES!". Personally, I received an Engineering degree in 1978, then an Architectural degree in 1976, then an Environmental Psychology degree in 1977 and then a Ministerial license in 1982. Had I chosen to go into the ministry when I was in my late teens, the answer would have been a big "NO!"

Receiving a "NO!" from a person you want to date, may propel you into the arms of the person you really should be spending your time with. *(Check out any Hallmark movie!)* Receiving a "NO!" from a job application, opens the doors to even greater possibilities than you may have imagined. I always congratulate anyone I meet who was recently fired from any job.

Receiving a "NO!" anytime in life has to be evaluated for the possible directions it MIGHT take you. If your "NO!" comes after much personal research, and/or a loud calling in your gut and/or a "this is the right time I know it" consideration, then you can decide to ignore it or not based on those criteria.

IGNORE THE "NO!"

HOW DO YOU KNOW WHEN TO IGNORE?

Saying "YES!" to the "NO!" comes back to our asking ourselves, "Why am I wanting to do this? Am I ignoring the obvious "NO!" out of pride or to be confrontational or do I really feel that what I am attempting to do will be the best action to take for me and all involved? To help us create the positive mind-set to be able to fully appreciate what we want out of a situation, I'd like to complete the acronym REBOOT which I introduced earlier in the book.

REBOOT came from my need to rehab my body and mind after my 2003 stroke. I introduced the first letter of the acronym from REBOOT earlier in this book. You will recall the first letter "**R**" stands for "<u>**Realize You Have Changed and You Can Never Be The Same**</u>."

Our mind remembers everything which happens to us in life; it is a perfect recording device. However, sometimes we may want to forget certain things. *But...forgetting does not change the fact that it happened!* We had an illness, we got a divorce, we lost a job, we declared bankruptcy. A friend betrayed us. Our child got in serious trouble. Whatever our experiences are, good or bad, they happened, and they cannot be changed. That becomes our history!

The second letter in the word REBOOT is **"E"** and it stands for "<u>**Expect Good from the Experience**</u>." If we take a deep look into all of our life experiences, we will notice that in many ways they mirror the educational process we go through as children. Each grade of school expands what we learned in the previous grade. And hopefully by the end of our formal schooling, we are able to more fully understand the world and how to maneuver all the twists and turns in it. It has been said that if we do not review and understand our history, we are destined to repeat it.

Rev. Dr. Stephen Albert

Do You Want the same "NOs!" Again?

The **"B"** in the word REBOOT stands for **"Believe in Your Ability to Overcome Challenges."** Most of those beliefs come from the less formal education that we received from everything else which we have done in our life. All the people we have met and all the opportunities we have encountered make up our history. Some challenges we have met well and others we would do differently if we had to do them over again. The fact that we can understand and differentiate them in that way, makes us more armed to meet similar future challenges.

The first **"O"** in the word REBOOT stands for **"Orient Yourself in Your New Life."** Just like moving into a new place to live, we need to choose what we will do with each room and how we plan to operate in our new environment. We know that there is a kitchen to place our groceries and a room to put the bed. What do we want on the walls? Sit down and write a list of what you want and how you want to think. The daily living in a new place offers us the chance to write a new chapter in our history book. There are many more chances to say "YES!" when we look into the mirror and smile.

The second **"O"** in the word REBOOT stands for **"Own Your New Life."** Whether we like it or not, WE created where we are in our life today. The consciousness we have had and the choices we have made, make us responsible for our present condition. And if an external factor, event or person, seems to have entered our history and created negative situations, WE need to recognize and deal with it as best we can. Become the cheerleader for YOU! And the cheer is "YES!"

The last letter in REBOOT is **"T"** and it stands for **"Test Yourself Constantly."** This offers us a chance to review the formal education we received in our youth as well as the informal life lessons that came through living our lives. How much have we retained? Remember when we learned to drive? Getting our driver's license and memorizing the rules was one thing; maneuvering on snow and ice for the first time in the winter, covered lessons which could only have been learned by being in the situation.

Ignore the "NO!"

And... if we need to learn more lessons, it is our responsibility to seek out the further education and experience needed to round our history. If we do not, we will hear a lot more "NO!" responses in the future.

So it is up to you! It is **ALWAYS** up to you!
Do you want "YES!" or "NO!" to dominate your life?

Are you ready to NOT shrink back when you encounter
a new goal for fear of it being impossible to reach?
Are you willing to move forward in life KNOWING
that you can accomplish much more
than what others limit you to?

Like a computer that is having troubles,
are you ready to **REBOOT yourself** away from "NO!"
and enjoy the wonders of "YES!"?

IGNORE the "NO!"
and begin a wonderful chapter in your History Book.

BE HAPPY! - BLESSINGS ALWAYS!

About the Author

Rev. Dr. Stephen Albert was born in Philadelphia and lived and worked in St. Louis and Phoenix before he settled in San Diego, California in 1989. He began teaching college classes and creating seminars to bring people of diverse backgrounds together in 1975. Steve has 4 college degrees including the Doctor of Religious Studies from Emerson Theological Institute.

Rev. Steve discovered the New Thought religion in 1989 and took over his first religious center in 1995. He met his wife, Rev. Dr. Abigail in 1999 and they led New Thought services in their center before embracing Interfaith in 2005. Since that time, they have devoted their efforts towards helping people realize the commonalities of all faiths and the need to honor and respect people of all backgrounds. In 2008 Steve authored the book, **The Interfaith Manual** which compares the New Thought faith with eleven other world faiths. In 2010, together with Abigail they co-authored **The Interfaith Workbook** which offers 40 weekly lessons to teach from for interfaith schools, religious centers and community classes.

Since his first book, **PEOPLEism** in 1986, Steve has authored 20 books and has taught in colleges since 1975. He created **'New Thought Day'** in 2012 which united the New Thought organizations throughout the world, and he did the groundwork to have

New Thought elevated to a 'World Faith' by the Multifaith Action Society. In 2010 Steve authored the E-Book, *From Religious to Spiritual; The New Thought Experience* and he and Abigail were asked to join the Advisory Board of the Association for Global New Thought. They also facilitated discussion groups at the 2012 AGNT Awakened World conference in Rome and Florence Italy. Steve designed the New Thought convention booth at the 2009 Parliament of the World's Religions conference in Melbourne Australia and at the PWR in Salt Lake City in 2015. He designed the 2018 New Thought Space at the PWR in Toronto, Canada.

In 2015, Steve took on the 2-year task of designing and developing the 'Connect' conference for the North American Interfaith Network and in 2017, over 250 people from over 20 different faiths attended the 5-day conference at UCSD in San Diego. The conference was so successful that it included a county celebration, **Interfaith Awareness Week,** which has now become a Global annual event the second week in August every year. Information can be obtained at their website:

https://world-interfaith.com

Many of Steve's books can be found on Amazon at:
https://www.amazon.com/Rev.-Albert/e/B088P7F8DG

Steve is a 2003 stroke survivor and has written about and counsels stroke victims and their families. He survived a 5-way, open-heart by-pass in 2012, gall bladder removal in 2016 and he received a replacement shoulder in 2020. Until COVID hit, Steve had been volunteering once a week in the Rehabilitation Center of Palomar Hospital since 2004.

Presently Steve is the Director of the World Interfaith Network which contains a database of Interfaith groups around the world. Over 36 presentations by interfaith groups and individuals are archived on the website **https://world-interfaith.com** and can be freely and easily accessed by the public.

Ignore the "NO!"

WIN Logo

For fun, Steve also likes to create interfaith artwork for the projects he works on.

Interfaith Eye Chart

Interfaith Stole

Endorsers Who Ignored The "NO!"

The three people who have endorsed the back of this book are individuals who "Ignored the NO!" and went beyond what others told them they could do. Their credentials are very extensive, and it is my honor to know then and to consider them good friends who are helping me to change the world for the better.

Ruth Broyde Sharone has been Honored internationally for her interfaith activism and leadership; filmmaker/journalist Ruth is the creator of "*INTERFAITH: The Musical.*" Ruth pioneered groundbreaking interfaith pilgrimages to the Middle East in the 90s, served as Co-Chair of the Southern California Parliament of the World's Religions for 10 years, and worked on the staff of the Global Parliament as well. She created a popular interfaith program on college campuses with her prize-winning documentary, "*God and Allah Need to Talk.*" Her riveting interfaith memoir, MINEFIELDS & MIRACLES, considered a "primer" on interfaith engagement, has received multiple literary awards and endorsements from 30 religious leaders including H.H. the Dalai Lama. Ruth also penned more than 70 articles for the on-line magazine, *The Interfaith Observer,* and co-authored the 2018 best-selling Amazon book, 21ST CENTURY VOICES: *Women Who Influence, Inspire, and Make A Difference.*

Rev. Wendy Craig-Purcell is the Author of "*Ask Yourself This*" and was ordained as a Unity Minister in 1980. Wendy helped design and participated in all three Assoc for Global New Thought-sponsored "Synthesis Dialogues," which brought together some of the world's leading thinkers to dialogue with His Holiness the Dalai Lama in Dharmsala, India. Additionally, her work with AGNT took her to Istanbul, Turkey as part of the planning for the Abraham Path Initiative and to Tokyo, Japan to present at the Goi Peace Foundation's Symposium on "Igniting the Divine Spark." She helped form the San Diego Department of Peace which has become Americans for the Department of Peace (AFDOP) and now encompasses all of Southern California. She is founder of the RacEquity360 (formerly known as The Anti-Racism Institute).

Dr. Barbara Fields is the Executive Director of The Association for Global New Thought. She is co-founder and project director of: The Gandhi King Seasons for Peace and Nonviolence (1998-present); the Synthesis Dialogues I, II, & III with His Holiness, the Dalai Lama of Tibet; and the omni-local initiatives for Harvard-based Abraham Walk Initiative in the Middle East. Formerly, she served as Program Director for the first Parliament of the World's Religions in Chicago, the Society for Buddhist-Christian Studies facilitated by Purdue University and was a delegate at the UNESCO Seminar on Religion and Peace in Granada, Spain. She has been Director/Producer of the Awakened World Conference Series 1999-2016, including the Gandhi King Peace Train, AGNT's Interfaith Forum in Rome/Florence, the Awakened World International Film Festival in Santa Barbara, CA and Symposium on Engaged Spirituality in San Diego. She is the author of AGNT's newest nine module activist curriculum: "Social Uplift Ministries" (S.U.M.)